P9-DFX-849

This book is a presentation of Weekly Reader Books. Weekly Reader Books offers book clubs for children from preschool through high school. For further information write to:
WEEKLY READER BOOKS, 4343 Equity Drive, Columbus, Ohio 43228

This edition is published by arrangement with Checkerboard Press.

Printed in the United States of America by Checkerboard Press.

WEEKLY READER BOOKS presents

A **Just Ask**™ Book

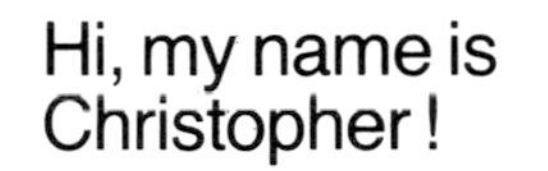

by Chris Arvetis
and Carole Palmer

illustrated by
James Buckley

FIELD PUBLICATIONS
MIDDLETOWN, CT.

Christopher!
Come on out.
It's snowing!
We're all here
to play.

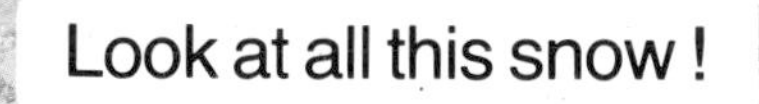
Look at all this snow !

Okay, Okay.
I see the snow!
But before we play
I want to find out–
why does it snow?

I have no idea.

I don't know.
Neither do I!

I don't either, but we could ask someone !

Can you tell us--
why does it snow?

I think I can.
Come into the house.
I'll show you a picture
to explain.

This is a cloud.
It is high up in the sky where it is very, very cold.

The cloud is made up of
tiny ice crystals and tiny
drops of water.

As the tiny drops of water become very, very cold, the drops stick to the ice crystals and freeze.

It's nice and warm in here !

Then the ice crystals get bigger and bigger.
We call them snowflakes.
As the snowflakes get bigger they get heavy, too.
Then they fall from the clouds.

If the air below the cloud is warm, the snowflakes turn into water and become rain.
If the air is cold, the snowflakes fall to the ground and it snows.

Let's go outside and see the snow.
Christopher, get dressed!

Look at the snowflakes.
Each one has six sides.
Some look like stars.
No two snowflakes are
ever exactly alike.
Look how pretty they are.

They're beautiful!

Sometimes it is very cold
and windy when it snows.
A lot of snow falls.
Then we have a *snowstorm*.
When the wind blows the
snow into large piles, we
have *snowdrifts*.

In big snowstorms, we use *snow shovels* and *snowplows* to clear the roads and paths.

Sometimes we use *snowshoes* to walk over the snow.

Others use *skis*.

Still others ride on *sleds* and *snowmobiles*.

And we can have fun in the snow
by making large *snowballs*
to make a *snowman*.

Just remember–
when the drops of water in
the clouds freeze and fall
to the ground, it snows.
Then we see–
snowflakes, snowstorms,
snowdrifts, snowplows,
and snowsuits.
And maybe even snowshoes,
snowmobiles, and a snowman.

And now I know
why it snows !